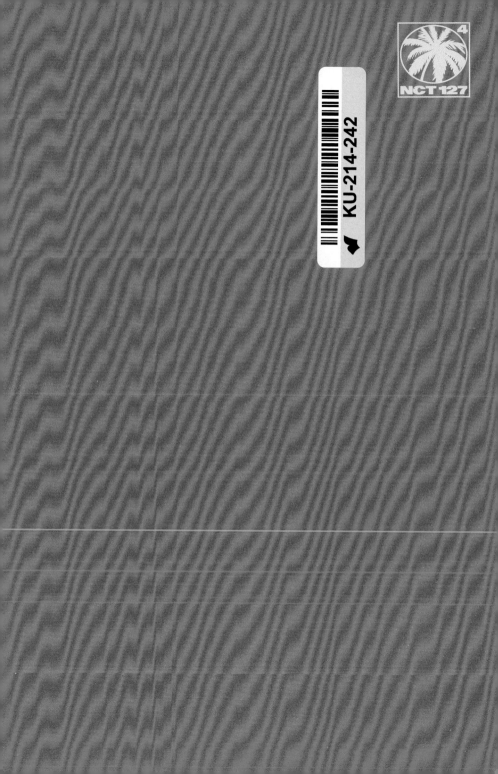

KU-214-242

NCT 127

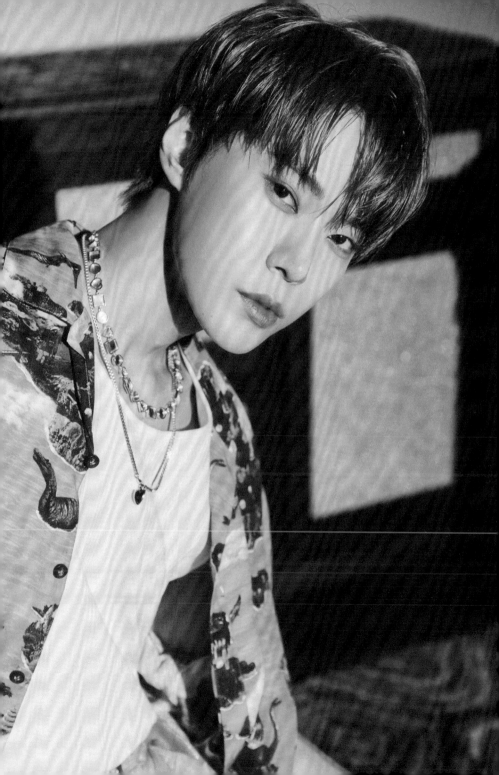

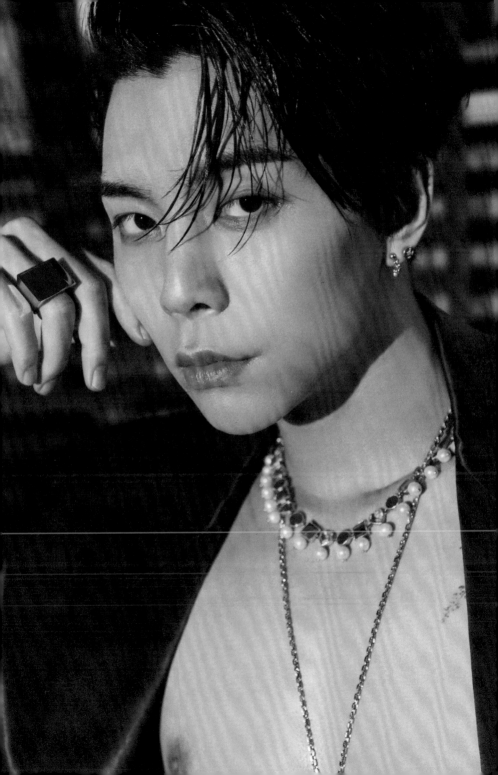

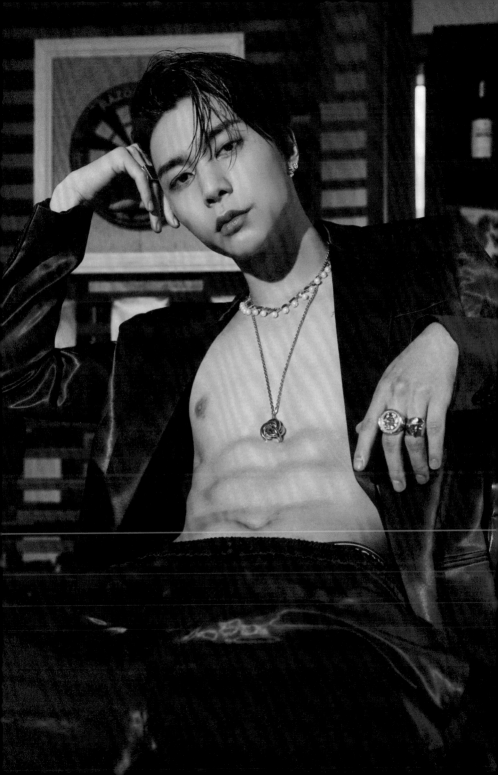

01
Faster

Korean Lyrics by	이송(VERYGOODS), 사하라(153/Joombas)
Composed by	Mich Hansen, Rasmus Hedegaard, Balance
Arranged by	Cutfather, Hedegaard

Vocal Directed by Rick Bridges, GDLO
Background Vocals by Balance, GDLO
Recorded by 우민정, 허준영 @ sound POOL studios,
이지홍 @ SM LVYIN Studio, 노민지 @ SM Yellow Tail Studio
Pro Tools Operating by GDLO
Digital Editing by 오병권, GDLO
Engineered for Mix by 이지홍 @ SM LVYIN Studio
Mixed by 정의석 @ SM Blue Cup Studio

Original Title: Faster
Original Writers: Mich Hansen / Rasmus Hedegaard / Balance
Original Publisher: Cutfather Publishing Limited (c/o Reservoir/
Reverb) / Copyright Control
Sub-Publisher: Fujipacific Music Korea Inc.

＊Fast 올라타는 My seat 준비됐지
My team 터질 듯한 엔진 Highway Fast
숨 막히는 열기 충돌할 듯 마치 끝이 없는
긴장 속에 Fast 우리만의 방식을 지켜내
Do or die always 'cause we ride on top
gear Fast all day 달려 울려 퍼질 함성
Checkered flag on my way
＊＊We're going Faster Faster we're
going Faster
Speed off high risk 한계를 pull off 출발선 위
완벽한 team work 내겐 없어 좌우도 오직 앞으로
다들 내 뒤로 huh 따라 할 수도 따라올 수도 없지
Thrill and more 미친 속도로 적당히가 안 돼 난
New record
＊Repeat
＊＊Repeat
내겐 없어 좌우도 오직 앞으로 다들 내 뒤로 huh
Faster 여기 주인공 맞아 우리 role pop the
champagne more going Faster
Kick off 끊김 없는 Focus 놓칠 틈 없지 Tension
계속해 매일 We don't have break 세게 자라온
Mental Fast like a flash huh and we the best all
지금부터 다시 Speed up 다시 Seat belt on and
we 앞서 널 그게 우리 몫

Fast 불이 붙어 My beat 준비됐지 My team 터질
듯한 엔진 Highway Fast 숨 막히는 열기 충돌할
듯 마치 끝이 없는 긴장 속에 Fast 우리만의
방식을 지켜내 Do or die always 'cause we ride
on top gear Fast all day 달려 울려 퍼질 함성
Checkered flag on my way
＊Repeat
타올라 Track 휘날려 Flag 터져 날 위한 축포
Faster race like the last one 계속 더 밟아 멈출
생각 없어 더 위로 Going Faster

02
질주 (2 Baddies)

Korean Lyrics by	sokodomo, 해일(Haeil), XINSAYNE
Composed by	Aron Bergerwall, Louise Lindberg, Tony Ferrari, Parker James,
	Moa "Cazzi Opeia" Carlebecker (Sunshine), Ellen Berg (Sunshine)
Arranged by	aron wyme
Additionally Arranged by	IMLAY

Vocal Directed by Maxx Song
Background Vocals by 이아일 (oiaisle)
Recorded by 강은지, 이지흥 @ SM SSAM Studio
Pro Tools Operating by Maxx Song
Digital Editing by 장우영 @ doobdoob Studio, Maxx Song,
강은지 @ SM SSAM Studio
Mixed by 정의석 @ SM Blue Cup Studio

Original Title: 2 Bitches 1 Porsche
Original Writers: Aron Bergerwall / Louise Lindberg /
Tony Ferrari / Parker James
Original Publishers: Mr Radar Music Group AB administered
by Kobalt Music Publishing Ltd (KMP) / TEN Songs AB
administered by Kobalt Music Publishing Ltd (KMP) /
Seven Summits Music / Tony Ferrari Publishing /
Songs by Parker (ASCAP)
Sub-Publishers: EKKO Music Rights (powered by CTGA) /
Universal Music Publishing Korea

Yes ah umm ah
2 Baddies 2 Baddies 1 Porsche 2 Baddies 2
Baddies 1 Porsche 몰라 난 네가 뭐라는지 있는
그대로의 멋을 봐 Don & Manner
One of a kind 파급은 나 Look in my eyes ya 내가
그린 기린 그림 속에서 move ya 창밖을 봐 문을
열어 바로 지금 ya I gotta go 시간은 gold we are
the next ya We pulling up and we cutting the
line 빛이 안 나 It isn't mine 타이밍 맞춰서 보이는
Sign open the keys open the mind Too fast ㅠㅠ
움직임은 blues clues Everybody jealous 따라
해보던가 New rules 위험한 생각에 맞서봐 이번엔
피하지 않아 난 Let's get away right now 더 빠르게
ya ya 그려낸 모습을 마주하게 Zero to 100 on the
highest speed 가는 길 앞엔 아무도 없지 내 삶은
나를 위한 고속도로 ay Fill up the tank pour that
gasoline on me rah

 ＊ 2 Baddies 2 Baddies 1 Porsche 2 Baddies
 2 Baddies 1 Porsche 몰라 난 네가 뭐라는지
 있는 그대로의 멋을 봐 Don & Manner
 2 Baddies 2 Baddies 1 Porsche 2 Baddies
 2 Baddies 1 Porsche 네가 날 본다면 알잖아
 우린 다채로운 색을 봐 Rainbow shade
Show me baby what's your style 최고를 느껴본
다음 너의 세상은 달라질 거야 You gon' wanna
come and wow 다른 건 필요 없어 자꾸만 화려해질

거야 넌 Now you wanna ride these wheels 우린
계속 타 너도 원하겠지 feel (원해 feel) yeah we got
no time to kill 배기음이 말해 많이 바빠 일 더 위로
가 점점 위로 가 널 잃지 마 끝까지 달려가 고민하지
마 불안할 뿐이야 Better get out of my way you
know

 ＊ Repeat
열린 도로 속에 하얗게 밝혀진 길이 여길 펼쳐 놔
가려진 세상에서 벗어나 Run through the highway
woah 끝이 없이 밟는 중 Wanna go to the moon
무한대로 baby 가속되는 소리 Nothing can stand in
our way ooh Zip zip show me zip it up what you
got (Hey Hey) Zip zip show me 주파수 맞추고
(Oh Hey) Vroom vroom noise 저리 가라고 (Hey)
Why don't we just drive away woah

 ＊ Repeat
na na na na na na na na Zip zip it z- zip it and
close na na na na na na na na 2 Baddies 1 Porsche
2 Baddies 2 Baddies 1 Porsche na na na na na na
na na Zip zip it z- zip it and close na na na na na
na na na na 2 Baddies 2 Baddies 1 Porsche

Korean Lyrics by	정하리(153/Joombas), 태용, 마크
Composed by	Dwayne "Dem Jointz" Abernathy Jr., Young Chance
Arranged by	Dem Jointz

Vocal Directed by 주찬양 (Pollen), Young Chance
Rap Making by NCT 태용, NCT 마크
Background Vocals by 주찬양 (Pollen)
Recorded by 강은지 @ SM SSAM Studio,
정유라 @ SM Starlight Studio
Digital Editing by 권유진 @ doobdoob Studio,
노민지 @ SM Yellow Tail Studio
Engineered for Mix by 이민규 @ SM Big Shot Studio
Mixed by 김철순 @ SM Blue Ocean Studio

Original Title: Fix It
Original Writer: Dwayne "Dem Jointz" Abernathy Jr.
Original Publisher: Dem Jointz Music administered by
Kobalt Music Publishing Ltd (KMP)
Sub-Publisher: EKKO Music Rights (powered by CTGA)

03
Time Lapse

시차 없는 꿈에 빛을 잃고 남아있는 Day and night 너를 불러봐도 닿지 않은 채 나 스스로 나를 가두어둔
밤 헤매는 이곳 긴 터널 같은 Soul 정신을 잃어 무의식에 끌려 너로 향해 선명하게 번진 시간 안에 yeah
yeah 혼자 두지 말아 줘 제발 I've killed time too many times report it's a murder case 끝이 없어 너의
glamour galore 이 현실을 꿈에 던져 Timeless timeless oh my god she got a timeless beauty 너의
눈빛은 나를 어지럽게 해 혼란을 주곤 해 But I really don't wanna waste our time yeah

    ＊Can we fix it baby can we fix it oh fix it 되감는 Dream
    반대로 돌아 너라는 시간
    Can we fix it baby can we fix it oh fix it 돌려 다시
    헤어날 수 없는 이 Time Lapse

번지는 환영과 닿아도 아무 느낌 없는 촉감만 눈 감고 그려보는 얼굴 난 미쳐가 끝없는 밤이 계속돼
다시 (yeah) 중력을 잃고 유영하는 듯 다시 거슬러 시간이란 틀을 벗어나 우리 함께 했던 기억만 Play
하루하루 매일 이렇게 견뎌 Everyday 아직도 너를 꿈꾸기를 반복해 또 널 꺼내 지워진 Face 그 안에
자꾸 바래져만 가는 시간을 잡아 oh it's you 아물지 않는 이 감각에 미쳐 All I need is you yeah

    ＊Repeat
애써 잊어보려 해도 반복돼 어둠과 빛이 구분도 안돼 더 아득해지는 기억 모두 꿈이었다고 내게 말해줘
No way 깨어 있어도 깨어날 수 없는 꿈 yeah Can we fix it baby can we fix it oh fix it 네가 없이 (Oh
can we fix it) 고장 난 시간 흐르지 않아 (네가 없이 난 oh)
Can we fix it (baby can we fix it) baby can we fix it oh fix it 돌려 다시 (다시 우릴)
헤어날 수 없는 이 Time Lapse

Korean Lyrics by	KENZIE
Composed by	KENZIE, IMLAY, JUNNY (주니)
Arranged by	KENZIE, IMLAY

Directed by KENZIE
Background Vocals by NCT 127
Recorded by 정유라 @ SM Starlight Studio
Digital Editing by 정유라 @ SM Starlight Studio
Mixed by 정유라 @ SM Starlight Studio

Original Title: On A Level
Original Writers: KENZIE / IMLAY / JUNNY
Original Publishers: EKKO Music Rights (powered by CTGA) / mauve company

04
불시착 (Crash Landing)

Yeah hmm look it's you I live for 꿈에서 널 만난다면 그건 내 wishlist 감춰놓았던 verse Hey I'm feelin' like I wanna keep you close 외딴섬에 우리 하루만이라도 yeah 아무 방해도 없는 낮과 밤들과 완벽한 고요 속에 우릴 내려놔 Imma make it last until the end 눈을 맞추고 (눈을 맞추고) 서로를 듣고 (서로를 듣고) 오 그럴 수 있다면 (Let us let us)

＊ Let us go to another planet 그 누, 그 누구도 몰래 누구도 몰래 말아야 Gotta fly on another level 눈에, 눈에 두 눈 속에 가득 차 있게 ah
＊＊ 멈춰버린 이곳의 시간들과 너를 편히 쉬게 할 공간도 All up all up into my love (On another new zone) 내가 만들게 해 줘 이 자리에

End of the world 우회해버린 별에 (ok) Steppin' my way up 잊혀진 우물 찾아내 홀로 핀 꽃 제멋대로 웃자라도 아름다운 땅 그 위에 우린

불시착 No better 어떤 순간 사건처럼 너를 만나 생각도 못 해본 걸 날 온통 뒤흔들어 버렸어 더는 돌이키지 못해 Can you feel my heart (Do you feel it now) Do you feel it now (oh baby hear that sound) Let us let us

＊ Repeat
＊＊ Repeat

yeah uh uh uh uh I get it for ya 사막을 다 적실 테니 나와 함께 갈래 별을 손에 줄 테니 나만 믿어 줄래 All my dreams in focus 이대로 흘러가 보는 거야 너와 나 그리고 시작해 One at a time baby I can't get enough ooh 눈에 눈에 너만 담아 Let us go to another planet 그 누, 그 누구도 몰래 That's just what I like oh 멈춰버린 이곳의 시간들과 (In this time) 너를 편히 쉬게 할 공간도 (oh no yeah yeah ho) All up all up into my love (On another new zone) 내가 만들게 해줘 이 자리에

05
Designer

Korean Lyrics by	김재원(JamFactory), 태용, 마크
Composed by	Corron Cole, James Bunton, Aaron Aye, Dwayne "Dem Jointz" Abernathy Jr., RYAN JHUN
Arranged by	No Past No Future, RYAN JHUN
Additionally Arranged by	Dem Jointz

Vocal Directed by Young Chance, 주찬양 (Pollen),
추대관, 서미래 (ButterFly)
Rap Making by NCT 태용, NCT 마크
Background Vocals by 주찬양 (Pollen)
Recorded by 정유라 @ SM Starlight Studio,
노민지 @ SM Yellow Tail Studio
Pro Tools Operating by 추대관, 서미래 (ButterFly)
Digital Editing by 권유진 @ doobdoob Studio,
이민규 @ SM Big Shot Studio
Mixed by 이민규 @ SM Big Shot Studio

Original Title: Desires Snippet
Original Writers: Corron Cole / James Bunton / Aaron Aye /
RYAN JHUN
Original Publishers: Holy Corron Music (BMI) /
Move JB Songs (BMI) / Audrey Allen Music (BMI) /
Marcan Entertainment
Sub-Publisher: Musikade

Yeah ay yeah ay yeah ay ay
　＊오감이 일렁여 나만이 느낀 Exclusive
　넌 나의 감성 I love it my Designer (More
　than perfect 작은 취향마저 best on me)
　누구도 못 가질 나만을 위한 Exclusive
　디테일마저 I love it my Designer (More
　than perfect 작은 취향마저 best on me)
내 세상에 녹아든 (to me) 이 감정은 Made by you
(by you) 완벽한 우리 둘 Pattern I think I'm in love
with you (I am) oh baby 넌 나에게 (나에게) 너만의
색을 입혀 매일 (color) 싫지 않아 다 이대로 좋아
(yeah) 더 짙어지게 칠해줄래 Mix and Match 어떤
방식도 OK Loose or tight 밀고 당겨도 OK (I don't
care) It's your eyes it's your smile it's your face
oh 전부 이끌려 갖고 싶어 Say more Classic 때로는
Dressy 섬세하게 다가와 Fit me (Come and fit me)
ay 맘을 Drawing 해 네가 느낀 대로 좀 더 깊어지는
눈빛에 빠져든 채로
　　＊ Repeat
나를 감싸와 빈틈 하나 없이 (You you) 네게 비친 나
It's perfect (It's alright, It's perfect, It's alright uh)
가장 특별한 너를 입을래 매일 I do every night
everyday yeah 내 맘의 무늬 (Yeah) 알아낸 Genie
(No) 얽히고설킨 시선의 끌림 (You and me) 내게

어울리잖아 그림같이 (and when I feel you imma
굳이 잘라 붙이고 재지 않아도 되지 이게 운명이면
(yeah) 내 전불 맡겨 (날 맡겨) 둘만의 Trend 속
(Trend) Let me follow (Let me follow) ay 안
놓칠게 I'm all in 자랑해 하루 종일 다른 건 필요 없어
Nothin' anything I want you got it girl
　　＊ Repeat
You're like my Designer I like a little tighter that's
my desire 내게로 come closer (baby I want you
all day all night) Meet me in rendezvous it's like
heaven 내가 못 느껴봤던 기분 yeah Out of bounds
침범하고 싶게 하지 너의 idea들을 보고 옮겨
sketching Crossing my mind walking like when
you're in Paris More than what I want 말해 뭐해
말아 you got You got what I need You got what I
like 사계절을 함께해도 바래지 않아 내게 변함없는
단 한 사람 그게 너야
　　＊ Repeat
　　＊＊ Oh oh oh oh oh oh Oh oh oh oh oh
　　Oh oh oh oh oh oh
　　＊＊ Repeat
You got it I love it Designer

06
윤슬 (Gold Dust)

Korean Lyrics by	이채영(JamFactory)
Composed by	Maureen "Mozella" McDonald, Nick Bradley, Stuart Crichton, Paul Blanco
Arranged by	Stuart Crichton, Paul Blanco

Vocal Directed by Young Chance, GDLO
Background Vocals by 이아일 (oiaisle)
Recorded by 권유진 @ doobdoob Studio,
노민지 @ SM Yellow Tail Studio, 정유라 @ SM Starlight Studio
Digital Editing by 정호진 @ sound POOL studios
Engineered for Mix by 이지홍 @ SM LVYIN Studio
Mixed by 남궁진 @ SM Concert Hall Studio

Original Title: Gold Dust
Original Writers: Maureen "Mozella" McDonald /
Nick Bradley / Stuart Crichton
Original Publishers: Mo Zella Mo Music / Karma Songs /
Budde Music UK / Native Tongue Music Publishing
Sub-Publishers: EMI Music Publishing Korea /
Fujipacific Music Korea Inc.

✱ 잘 자 내 달빛 이리 와서
안겨 깊숙이 밤이 수 놓인
잔물결 위로 누워
아마 너는 모르지 얼마나
네 빛이 예쁜지
금세 잔뜩 닿아 반짝이잖니
금색 길을 내어 나를
빛내지
널 만나기 전엔 그저 어두웠지
칠흑 같은 바다 밑을 본 적 있니
일렁이는 얼굴 표정 없는 매일
괜히 흘러갈 뿐 기대 없던
내일 그런 어느 날 내 위로
쏟아지던 은하수 안녕하고선
빤히 날 바라보는 눈망울 그제야
눈치챘어 손에 물든 빛 별이 뜬 게
아냐 이건 너야 짙은 밤 내게 와서
너를 새기던 길 금빛이 된 바다
달이 떴네 시간이 멈춘 것 같았던
그 즈음 단번에 널 떠올리곤 이게
사랑일까 해
　　✱ Repeat

물기 어린 내음 고갤 들게 해
어김없이 생긋 웃어주는 너 nah
nah 왜일까 네게서 바다 향이
어젯밤 나에게 묻은 건지 코끝을
맴도네 Give it to me give it to me
오늘도 다시 올까 소란한 그 빛
벌써 스러져가 아득한데 감은 눈
뜨면 순간 너와 하늘이길 금빛
길을 따라 네게 갈게 (Yeah)
　　✱ Repeat
무한하게 반짝여 넌 Like magic
그 환함에 전부 다 잊어 Bad
things 그런 너를 좋아해 이미
알지 꿈에서도 아른거리는 달빛
oh ah oh ah 어디 한번 물어봐
파도 위에 손 대봐 고요하던
물결이 요동치는 것을 봐 오직
널 향해 흘러 그 중력의 힘에 내
바다가 다 말라도
잘 자 내 달빛 이리 와서 안겨
깊숙이 밤이 수 놓인 잔물결 위로
누워 아마 이제 알겠지 얼마나

네 빛이 예쁜지 금세 잔뜩 닿아
반짝이잖니 금색 길을 내어 나를
빛내지 Gold Dust up my sea
금색 가룰 뿌려 찬란히 밤이 수
놓인 잔물결 위에 뿌려 아마 이제
알겠지 얼마나 네 빛이 예쁜지
금세 잔뜩 닿아 반짝이잖니 금색
길을 내어 나를 빛내지

Korean Lyrics by	오현선(lalala studio)
Composed by	Rokman (The Hello Group), Lauren Dyson (The Hello Group), Sean Fischer (Honua)
Arranged by	Rokman, Sean Fischer

Vocal Directed by Young Chance
Background Vocals by NCT 도영, NCT 해찬
Recorded by 권유진, 이정빈 @ doobdoob Studio
Digital Editing by 권유진 @ doobdoob Studio
Engineered for Mix by 강은지 @ SM SSAM Studio
Mixed by 정의석 @ SM Blue Cup Studio

Original Title: Black Clouds
Original Writers: Charles Frank Rhodes / Lauren Dyson / Sean Fischer
Original Publishers: THG Publishing / Honua Music / Tel Ray Publishing administered by Kobalt Music Publishing Ltd (KMP)
Sub-Publishers: Sony Music Publishing Korea / EKKO Music Rights (powered by CTGA)

07
흑백 영화 (Black Clouds)

Woah oh yeah 하필 우산조차 없는 날 갑작스럽게 머리 위로 드리운 Black Clouds 오랜 필름 같은 Background 흑백 영화 같아 yeah 요즘 넌 어떤지 I can't take it 뜨겁던 손끝이 식어가지 yeah 봐 Monotone인 세상엔 늘 함께했던 우린 없어 마치 꿈을 꾸는 듯이 먼 기억 속의 우릴 소리 없이 부르면

    ✻ 너와 날 물 들이는 Rain 회색에 젖을 때
    널 그릴 때 우리 영화는 시작돼
    비처럼 무채색이 돼 펼쳐질 장면에
    가득한 건 오직 너와 하늘을 채운 Black Clouds

Rain rain like a filter 왠지 색다른 일이 일어날 것 같은 걸 고개를 돌린 순간 지붕 아래 앉아서 비를 피한 네가 보여 놀란 듯 두 눈이 커다랗지 때마침 구름이 일렁이지 어색한 나의 인사에 동시에 웃음꽃이 번져 너와 닿았었던 Ending 그 뒤에 남은 얘기 이어지는 Epilogue 시간이 지나도 바래지 않을 너와 나의 순간 깊어지는 명암 선명하게 우릴 채워가

    ✻ Repeat
    ✻✻ Rain rain up in my head 흑백 영화 속에 너와 내가 가득해
    Rain rain always be there 우리들의 이야기 끝이 없게

우산이 없어도 괜찮은 이유 널 마주한 지금 흠뻑 젖어도 좋을 듯해 잠시 멈추고픈 밤 손을 잡은 너와 나 어깨를 감싸주는 Rain 기억에 젖을 때 되감을 때 우리 영화는 영원해 이대로 발을 맞춘 채 나란히 걸을래 눈앞엔 선명한 너와 하늘을 채운 Black Clouds

    ✻✻ Repeat

With the Black Clouds with the Black Clouds with the Black Clouds 너와 날 위한 Black Clouds

Korean Lyrics by	이창혁(JamFactory)
Composed by	Oneye, Andreas Öberg, Johan Gustafsson
Arranged by	Oneye, Johan Gustafsson

Vocal Directed by 추대관, 서미래 (ButterFly), GDLO
Background Vocals by 주찬양 (Pollen)
Recorded by 이지홍 @ SM LVYIN Studio,
노민지 @ SM Yellow Tail Studio
Pro Tools Operating by 추대관, 서미래 (ButterFly), GDLO
Digital Editing by 우민정, 이지홍 @ SM LVYIN Studio
Mixed by 이지홍 @ SM LVYIN Studio

Original Title: Playback
Original Writers: Oneye / Johan Gustafsson / Andreas Öberg
Original Publishers: The Kennel AB /
Universal Music Publishing AB / Deep Cut Publishing
Sub-Publishers: Universal Music Publishing Korea /
Soundgraphics admin by Music Cube, Inc.

08
Playback

Playback 난 왜 톱니바퀴처럼 반복된 말을 해
또 습관처럼 늘 같은 행동 언제나 너를 찾는
변함없는 태도 yeah 넌 없는데 I don't know
여전해 함께했던 게 전부 망상 같아 아쉬운
기억 속 추억 속 너야 언제나 수없이 되뇌이지
쳇바퀴는 돌아가고 결국 다시 그 안에서 뛰고
있어 지금 난
　　＊ Playback 네가 끝없이 보여 왜 이래
　　되풀이돼 매 순간
　　머릿속에 나타나는 넌 Deja vu 다 잊고
　　비워내도 늘 그때 뿐
　　Playback 다시 한번 네 모습을 재생
　　돌아가는 태엽처럼
　　이 순간 끝없이 맴돈 너의 이름 That
　　Playback Playback yeah
들리는 음악이 왜 yeah everytime 선명한 음성이
돼 yeah 날 찾아 난 똑같은 끌림으로 또 널 만나지
woah I want it 너의 온기 너는 어디나 있어 날
찾아와 다시 매번 돌고 돌아 왜 이럴까 왜 이럴까
woah 쳇바퀴 속 뛰고 있어 지금까지 멈춤 없이
밤을 새며 매 순간

　　＊ Repeat
　　＊＊ Take me back take me take me
take me back take me
Take me back take me take me take
me back (Playback)
Take me back take me take me take
me back take me
Playback Playback yeah
시간이 약이 될 순 없나 봐 (그런가봐) Could we
do it one more time oh woah Play ba ba ba ba
ba ba ba back I want you playback
Playback 네가 끝없이 보여 왜 이래 되풀이돼
매 순간 (We gon' playback playback we gon'
stay back stay back) 머릿속에 나타나는 넌 Deja
vu (너는 Deja vu) 다 잊고 비워내도 늘 그때 뿐
(늘 그때 뿐) Playback 다시 한번 기억들을 재생
돌아가는 태엽처럼 (We gon' playback playback
we gon' stay back stay back) 이 순간 끝없이
맴돈 너의 이름 That Playback Playback yeah
　　＊＊ Repeat

09
Tasty (貘)

Korean Lyrics by	조윤경
Composed by	Teodor Herrgård, Rebecca Sjöberg, Gustav Nilsson,
	Moa "Cazzi Opeia" Carlebecker (Sunshine), Ellen Berg (Sunshine)
Arranged by	Teodor Herrgård, Rebecca Sjöberg, Gustav Nilsson

Vocal Directed by Noday, 주찬양 (Pollen)
Background Vocals by 이아일 (oiaisle)
Recorded by 강은지 @ SM SSAM Studio, 정유라 @ SM Starlight Studio
Digital Editing by 장우영 @ doobdoob Studio,
정유라 @ SM Starlight Studio
Mixed by 정유라 @ SM Starlight Studio

Original Title: So Tasty
Original Writers: Teodor Herrgårdh / Rebecca Sjöberg /
Gustav Nilsson
Original Publishers: The Kennel AB /
Universal Music Publishing AB
Sub-Publisher: Universal Music Publishing Korea

불은 전부 꺼 모두 쉿 쉽게 잠들기엔 Dream in the big bad zoo 까마득히 먼 In the mood 의미 없이 세어 봐 넌 sheep one two We're savage outlaws rock solid no flaws 어둠 속에 붉게 빛나는 시선 가득히 노려 Bite of the sweet sweet 유심히 찾던 Villain in the dark 노려 난 Strike 불안한 네 악몽을 찢고 등장해 My bike We're savage outlaws rock solid no flaws 네 오싹한 꿈은 제법 구미가 당겨 babe 활개 쳐 대던 goblin 휙 낚아채고 입꼬리를 올린 a king on a throne 묘한 눈빛은 crazy 날카로운 손 I swear it's Tasty like butter on scones

✳ Like chili so hot I'm hunting nightmares I want it (So Tasty) 꽤 짜릿한 맛 소름이 오싹 I want it (So Tasty) 네 꿈을 노려 누가 감히 한 번 자극해 봐 어디 yeah I want it (So Tasty) 너의 모든 밤이 이젠 감미로운 Honey you can have it (So Tasty)

I'm in the big bad 깨물어 Cling clang Make a boom 돼 줄게 나쁜 꿈에 날린 Boomerang 소스라쳐 깨 A.M. 6 토해내듯 거친 Breath 사라진 핏기 깨질 듯 뒤엉킨 기억 사이 그 잔상마저 Bang 거칠게 몰아 Move Cause we're savage outlaws rock solid no flaws 보란 듯이 세운 이 이리 온 착하지 Just eat it eat it eat it 널 기다리는 Billion in the light 마땅히

다 (Gonna strike) 네 몫인 아름다운 꿈을 향해 ride my bike (I ride my bike) Cause we're savage outlaws rock solid no flaws 늘 반복 되던 악몽은 날 기다린 축제 (Just make a move) 풀린 광기는 crazy yeah I'm in the zone I swear it's Tasty like butter on scones

✳ Repeat

깊이 잠들어 아침이면 넌 아무것도 넌 모를 걸 괴로웠던 꿈을 내게 맡길 때 너를 지켜내는 그 맛 I like that yeah So Tasty So Tasty uh uh uh uh uh yeah yeah yeah yeah yeah yeah yeah So Tasty

✳ Repeat

We're savage outlaws rock solid no flaws Like chili so hot I'm hunting nightmares I want it (So Tasty) (Bring it back now) We're savage outlaws (Let's go) rock solid no flaws 넌 잠이 들고 난 깨어나 곧 네 꿈은 So Tasty

10
Vitamin

Korean Lyrics by	김예인(JamFactory)
Composed by	Jacob Attwooll, Jon Eyden, Eben
Arranged by	Jacob Attwooll

Vocal Directed by 주찬양 (Pollen), Young Chance
Background Vocals by 주찬양 (Pollen)
Recorded by 이민규 @ SM Big Shot Studio,
정유라 @ SM Starlight Studio, 우민정 @ sound POOL studios
Digital Editing by 안창규, 이민규 @ SM Big Shot Studio
Mixed by 이민규 @ SM Big Shot Studio

Original Title: Vitamin E
Original Writers: Jacob Attwooll / Jonathan Eyden Ross /
Eben (Eben Franckewitz)
Original Publishers: Cooking Vinyl Publishing Ltd /
Warner Chappell Music Scandinavia AB / Club Colbat Music
Sub-Publisher: Warner Chappell Music Korea Inc.

yee yeah Girl you got that take it all baby and I'll
be the therapist for the day that's ok yeah hoo
Hey babe 나를 삼켜 일단 너의 기분 전부 바꿔 난
예고 없이 몰아치던 무거운 그 무력감 (Ok) 그 속에
갇힌 너를 꺼낼 Time yeah 뭐든 말해 Telling me
힘겨워 말아 내게 덜어놔 널 괴롭힐 통증 따윈 없게
네가 바란 Medicine 어차피 나일 테니 이리 와 이리
저 햇살을 빌려와 따스한 빛 밀려와 어두워진 너의
어깰 비출 수 있게 지칠 땐 Fresh한 곳을 찾아 Chill
흐렸던 Your eyes 반짝 빛나도록

      ＊ Vitamin me Vitamin me
      너를 채울 단 한 알의 Vitamin me
      Multi Vitamin me try it and see
      전부 줄 수 있어 baby Vitamin me
      Vitamin me Vitamin me
      나로 채워 너의 결핍 Vitamin me
      Multi vitamin me ABCD 뭐든 되어 줄게
      baby Vitamin me (ah woo)
어떤 맛을 좋아해 뭐든 골라 어떤 말투 너를 또 웃게
할까 모든 게 쉽진 않아도 좋아 나를 볼 때 넌 힘이
막 넘쳐 yeah 가파른 호흡의 원인이 나란 걸 잘 알지
과도한 작용 계속돼 너도 나의 Vitamin 더없이 서롤
가득 채우지 yeah 어지러운 바람에 휘청이고 있을 때
나의 손을 잡아 함께 걸을 수 있게 네 손에 날 꽉 쥐여

줄 테니 힘들 땐 날 다 털어 가져가봐
      ＊ Repeat
눈 뜨면 제일 먼저 나를 찾아 너의 하루에 내가 없인
안될 듯이 네가 먼저 나를 찾고 있잖아 Just take a
bite of me
      ＊ Repeat
      ＊＊ Vi-vi-vitamin me Vi-vi-vitamin me-
      me Vi-vi-vitamin vitamin me Vi-vi-
      vitamin me-me
      ＊＊ Repeat

11
LOL (Laugh-Out-Loud)

Korean Lyrics by	이혜윰(JamFactory)
Composed & Arranged by	Fabian Torsson, Harry Sommerdahl, Albin Nordqvist

Vocal Directed by 서미래 (ButterFly), 주찬양 (Pollen)
Background Vocals by 주찬양 (Pollen)
Recorded by 허준영, 우민정 @ sound POOL studios
Pro Tools Operating by 서미래 (ButterFly)
Digital Editing by 정호진 @ sound POOL studios,
이지효 @ SM LVYIN Studio
Mixed by 이지홍 @ SM LVYIN Studio

Original Title: Bangin'
Original Writers: Fabian Torsson / Harry Sommerdahl /
Albin Nordqvist
Original Publishers: EKKO Music Rights Europe (powered
by CTGA) / The Kennel AB / Universal Music Publishing AB /
Cosmos Music Publishing
Sub-Publishers: EKKO Music Rights (powered by CTGA) /
Universal Music Publishing Korea / Music Cube, Inc.

Ooh yeah oh ha listen to a little bit of this 딱히 웃을 만한 일도 요샌 많지 않아 (잘 웃지 않아) 뭐든 시큰둥한 (That's right) 표정을 하고 있어 다 마음대로 안 돼 어쩌겠어 (됐어) 흘러가는 쪽으로 흐르게 둬 또 툭툭 털어내고 일어나 (Life) 넘어져도 뭐 어때 So fine (yeah) 괜찮아 다 별거 아닌 (Hey) 시시한 농담 그런 얘기로 (That's right) 널 듣고 있으면 (That's right) 난 미소가 번져 This time we'll spend this time together 항상 같은 자릴 지켜준 (That's right) 고마워 난 그게 너라서 You know it's true

　　＊ 더 크게 웃어 Laugh it up laugh it up 네 고민들은 구석에다 던져 놔
　　웃고 떠들어대 우린 LOL 지친 마음 속의 너를 꺼내어
　　오늘을 즐겨 다른 생각은 마 웃을 때가 누구보다 빛나
　　천 마디 위로보다 이 순간 (More) 더 크게 Smile

Ooh Just like we do Hey wait a minute let me tell ya yeah 손과 발을 맞춰 우리만의 제스처 리듬을 더 느껴 (Hey) (꽉 찬 머릿속은 비워) 어떤 말없이도 알고 있어 우리끼린 (Like) 퍼즐 위에 딱 맞는 느낌 (Hey) (That's right) 많은 거 안 바래 I'm not at all 그저 지금 같기만 해 yeah that's what's up 깊숙이 간직해 둔 Beautiful mind 언제든 꺼내 돌아갈 수 있으니까 행복은 늘 가까웠지 Whenever you call 힘든 날이면 난 너를 찾아가 (That's right) 넌 나를 찾아와 This time we'll spend this time together 항상 같은 자릴 지켜준 (That's right) 고마워 난 그게 너라서 (You know it's true)

　　＊ Repeat

Ooh 언제나 Night and day (All night and day) 'Cause we belong together (Ooh we belong) 지금처럼 Forever 함께면 웃음이 멎질 않지 (Smiling) 코드가 맞아 딱 (Kind of vibe) 조금 지친 날에도 괜찮아 한 걸음 쉬어가 yeah

　　＊ Repeat

na na na (that's right) na na na na na (yeah yeah ooh ooh) na na na (that's right 웃어 볼래) Just like we do na na na (that's right) na na na na na 걱정 마 모두 잘 될 거니까 (More) 더 크게 Smile

12
1, 2, 7 (Time Stops)

Korean Lyrics by	박성희(JamFactory)
Composed by	Peter Wallevik, Daniel Davidsen, Iain James
Arranged by	PhD

Vocal Directed by 주찬양 (Pollen), 추대관, GDLO, 서미래 (ButterFly)
Background Vocals by 주찬양 (Pollen)
Recorded by 정유라 @ SM Starlight Studio, 이지홍 @ SM LVYIN Studio, 노민지 @ SM Yellow Tail Studio
Pro Tools Operating by 추대관, GDLO, 서미래 (ButterFly)
Digital Editing by 노민지 @ SM Yellow Tail Studio
Mixed by 김철순 @ SM Blue Ocean Studio

Original Title: Time Stops
Original Writers: Peter Wallevik / Daniel Davidsen / Iain James
Original Publishers: Wallevik Music AB administered by Kobalt Music Publishing Ltd (KMP) / Kobalt Music Services Ltd (KMS) administered by Kobalt Music Publishing Ltd (KMP) / BMG Rights Management (UK) Limited
Sub-Publishers: EKKO Music Rights (powered by CTGA) / Fujipacific Music Korea Inc.

달이 비춘 거리 위 This evening
쉬어 갈 틈이 없는 Fast track
in my life 시간도 시간에 쫓긴 채
yeah 게으를 줄을 몰라 So fast
시곌 멈출 방법이 있어 단 한
가지 살짝 눈 감아 난 천천히
네게 알려줄 테니

＊1 2 and maybe
7 o'clock 너와 함께
하는 Time 세상은
Stops When I'm with
you baby 4 5 6 or
11 o'clock hey
꿈속 Night 꿈 밖의
Day 네 순간은 내
기억 속에 Stop
＊＊ You make time
just stop you make
time stop

스물네 조각의 시간으로 이은
1 day 빼곡해 완벽해 다른 건
I don't mind yeah 네 미소
또는 눈물 어린 모든 Time
원해 Press pause 원해 Press

rewind Girl you're shaking
and breaking me 우린 원이
되니까 넌 나의 끝이자 나의
모든 Start 네 1초를 나에게
줄래 더 오래 함께 할게 난 ah

＊ Repeat
＊＊ Repeat
네 손등만 스쳐도 My heart
stops beating 언제나 이
순간처럼 함께한 Dreaming
꿈으로 그린 I I 지금 우리 I I
couldn't change you even if I
could I couldn't 또 내 마음은
Won't stop (won't stop) 엎어
모래시계 When it drops (when
it drops) 멈춰 세운 Sky yeah
I feel I high 네 1초, 2초 간직
할게 다 Don't say a word
시침의 발을 멈춰 세운 밤 (Oh
이 밤) 같은 꿈 그 안의 Fantasy
Don't say a word 늘 시간보다
우린 천천히 (Right here next
to me) 순간을 찬란히
＊ Repeat

＊＊ Repeat
Girl you make time stop girl
you make time stop
When I'm with you baby you
make time stop

NCT 127
THE 4TH ALBUM
CREDITS

Executive Producer   SM ENTERTAINMENT Co., Ltd.
Producer   SOO-MAN LEE
Music & Sound Supervisor   YOO YOUNG JIN

Producing Director
이성수

A&R Director
채정희
A&R Direction & Coordination
고아라, 이종원, 이지훈
International A&R
송소민, 채정균, 최유준
Music Licensing
오정은, 손연주, 이루리

Recorded by
이민규 @ SM Big Shot Studio
이지홍 @ SM LVYIN Studio
정유라 @ SM Starlight Studio
노민지 @ SM Yellow Tail Studio
강은지 @ SM SSAM Studio
우민정 @ sound POOL studios
허준영 @ sound POOL studios
장우영 @ doobdoob Studio
권유진 @ doobdoob Studio
이정빈 @ doobdoob Studio

Mixed by
남궁진 @ SM Concert Hall Studio
김철순 @ SM Blue Ocean Studio
정의석 @ SM Blue Cup Studio
이민규 @ SM Big Shot Studio
이지홍 @ SM LVYIN Studio
정유라 @ SM Starlight Studio

Mastered by
권남우 @ 821 Sound Mastering

Creative Director
박준영

Art Director
조우철
Creative Concept Planning & Graphic Design
이소희, 조우식
Photography
이준경
Set Design
전민규
Mood Sampler Direction & Arrangement
이소희, 조우식
Mood Sampler Director
신태석

Artist Content Director
이상민

Music Video Direction & Arrangement
김기현, 허은지
Music Video Director
Jinooya Makes
Content & eXperience (CX)
유지이, 최은정, 최우림
Promotion Video Director
홍재환, 이혜수
Content & Promotion (CP)
신다정, 정은비, 김혜민, 박수현
SMCU Development
모나리, 김지은
Digital Content Development
Steven M. Lee

Artist Visual Planning
김소연
Styling
김영진
Hair
한송희
Make-Up
안성은

Performance Director
홍성용
Performance Creative
사지웅, 김효진
Choreography Direction
염희섭
Choreographer
Rie Hata, Anthony Lee, Keone Madrid, Taryn Cheng, 이바다, PREPIX_iLL

<Official Homepage>

SM ENTERTAINMENT Official Homepage   http://www.smtown.com

<Social Network Service>

Instagram	www.instagram.com/nct127
Twitter	www.twitter.com/NCTsmtown_127
Facebook	www.facebook.com/NCT127.smtown
Weibo	https://weibo.com/NCT127smtown

<YouTube Channel>

www.youtube.com/nctsmtown

www.youtube.com/nct127

www.youtube.com/smtown

Management Director
강병준

Artist Management & Promotion
이원균, 김선호, 박성호, 정민혁, 강명구,
문광현

Communication Center
김대빈, 강희목, 유아름, 전애정, 박민정

Artist Development Director
윤희준

Artist Planning & Development
조유은, 신평화

Media Planning
김민성, 김호식, 김인환, 복민권, 허재혁

Marketing Director
김지원
Public Relations & Publicity
정상희, 이지선, 임현정
FC Management
이정아, 이진화

Global Business Director
최정민
Global Management & Promotion
유은정, 강성은, 정한나

Digital Distribution
정지혜, 이가영, 민혜민, 이수영, 장혜림,
박서영, 김희정, 최지용

Product Management
진현주
Recorded Distribution
여원규, 김지영, 이상형

[SM USA]
A&R Direction & Coordination
Janie Yoo, Victor Portillo, Emily J. Oh

[SM CHINA]
Managing & Marketing Director
이우용
Record & Digital Distribution
권진희, 서지예, 장희수, 장은정
Marketing & Promotion
이희성, 사문, 임성택

[SM SEA]
Managing & Marketing Director
한경진
Marketing & Promotion
원경재

[Stream Media Corporation INC.]
Managing & Marketing Director
김동우

Executive Supervisor
이성수, 탁영준